DISCARD

Westminster Public Library
3705 W. 112th Ave.
Westminster, CO 80031
www.westminsterlibrary.org

Pebble®
Plus

Lightning

by Erin Edison

Consulting Editor: Gail Saunders-Smith, PhD

CAPSTONE PRESS
a capstone imprint

Pebble Plus is published by Capstone Press,
1710 Roe Crest Drive, North Mankato, Minnesota 56003.
www.capstonepub.com

Copyright © 2012 by Capstone Press, a Capstone imprint. All rights reserved.
No part of this publication may be reproduced in whole or in part, or stored in a retrieval system, or transmitted in any
form or by any means, electronic, mechanical, photocopying, recording, or otherwise, without written permission of the
publisher. For information regarding permission, write to Capstone Press,
1710 Roe Crest Drive, North Mankato, Minnesota 56003.

 Books published by Capstone Press are manufactured with paper
containing at least 10 percent post-consumer waste.

Library of Congress Cataloging-in-Publication Data
Edison, Erin.
 Lightning / by Erin Edison.
   p. cm.—(Pebble plus. Weather basics)
 Summary: "Simple text and full-color photographs describe lightning and how it forms"—Provided by publisher.
 Includes bibliographical references and index.
 ISBN 978-1-4296-6058-7 (library binding)
 ISBN 978-1-4296-7078-4 (paperback)
 1. Lightning—Juvenile literature. I. Title. II. Series.
 QC966.5.E35 2012
 551.56'32—dc22   2010053977

Editorial Credits
Erika L. Shores, editor; Kyle Grenz, designer; Laura Manthe, production specialist

Photo Credits
Alamy: Horizon International Images Limited, 11; Getty Images Inc.: Photographer's Choice/Steven Hunt, 21, Stone
Ralph H Wetmore II, 13, Visuals Unlimited/Thomas Wiewandt, 19, Workbook Stock/Samuel D. Barricklow, 17;
Shutterstock: Andraž Cerar, back cover, James "BO" Insogna, front cover, Jhaz Photography, 1, 5, 7, 15, valdezrl, 9

Artistic Effects
Shutterstock: marcus55

**Capstone Press thanks Mike Shores, earth science teacher at RBA Public Charter School
    in Mankato, Minnesota, for his assistance on this book.**

Note to Parents and Teachers

The Weather Basics series supports national science standards related to earth science. This
book describes and illustrates lightning. The images support early readers in understanding
the text. The repetition of words and phrases helps early readers learn new words. This book
also introduces early readers to subject-specific vocabulary words, which are defined in the
Glossary section. Early readers may need assistance to read some words and to use the Table of
Contents, Glossary, Read More, Internet Sites, and Index sections of the book.

Printed in the United States of America in North Mankato, Minnesota.
112011   006464R

Table of Contents

What Is Lightning?

Bright flashes light up the sky.

Big jagged streaks hit the ground.

A summer storm has

brought lightning.

Lightning is a kind of electricity.
Storm clouds carry water droplets
and ice crystals. The tiny particles
bump into one another.
They make electricity in the clouds.

As the electricity becomes
stronger, lightning flashes.
Lightning is how clouds
get rid of electricity.

9

Lines of lightning are called bolts.
They can be 10 miles
(16 kilometers) long. They can be
54,000 degrees Fahrenheit
(30,000 degrees Celsius).

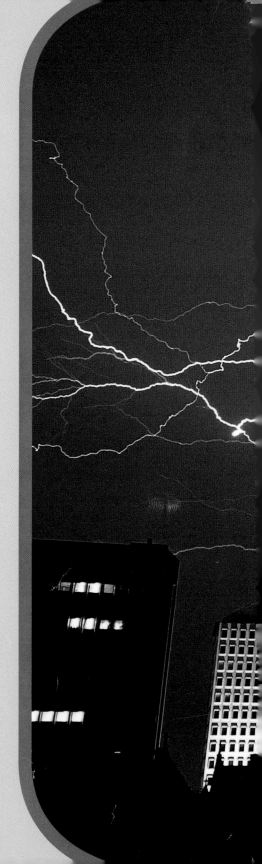

11

Kinds of Lightning

Ribbon lightning looks
like jagged streaks.
It darts from the sky
toward the ground.

Forked lightning also goes
from a cloud toward
the ground. It looks like
an upside-down tree.

Lightning doesn't always shoot toward the ground. Sheet lightning streaks inside a cloud. Lightning bolts also jump from cloud to cloud.

Crash and Boom

Thunder is the sound of lightning heating the air. A loud crash means lightning is close. Many booms mean lightning is far away.

Stay Safe

Lightning is dangerous.

Stay indoors during thunderstorms.

If you're caught outside

during a storm, stay away

from trees and power lines.

Glossary

bolt—a line of lightning coming out of a cloud

electricity—a form of energy caused by moving particles

particle—a tiny piece of something

thunder—the sound made when lightning heats the air

Read More

Flanagan, Alice K. *Thunder and Lightning.* Weather Watch. Mankato, Minn.: Child's World, Inc., 2010.

Goldsmith, Mike. *The Weather.* Now We Know About. New York: Crabtree Pub., 2010.

Salas, Laura Purdie. *Colors of Weather.* Colors All Around. Mankato, Minn.: Capstone Press, 2011.

Internet Sites

FactHound offers a safe, fun way to find Internet sites related to this book. All of the sites on FactHound have been researched by our staff.

Here's all you do:

Visit *www.facthound.com*

Type in this code: 9781429660587

Super-cool stuff! Check out projects, games and lots more at **www.capstonekids.com**

Index

Word Count: 178

Grade: 1

Early-Intervention Level: 18

Westminster Public Library
3705 W. 112th Ave.
Westminster, CO 80031
www.westminsterlibrary.org